No Longer Defined

Shannon Poteet

BookLeaf Publishing

Presentation by *BookLeaf Publishing*

Web: www.bookleafpub.com

E-mail: info@bookleafpub.com

ISBN: 9789357212144

First edition 2023

DEDICATION

To those who know me, and love me anyway...

M-A-double T

They said they would walk me out,
But he backs me into the stairs,
His friend stands in the shadows,
It's dark and no one can hear.

We descent to the bottom,
It smells yellow and cold,
Too much alcohol, he sways
I am not yet afraid of being alone.

I don't understand him, nor his quiet friend,
They both edge closer,
He tells me there's nothing I can do if he wants
to take,
Nothing to stop him from making me his next
mistake.

I brandish a blade,
It won't cut tape.
He steps forward -
He stumbles, he grins -
He raises his arm, glaring at me again -
I can't move. Is this what it's like to lose your
own life?
No. He's still smiling.
It must be a joke I just don't know how to take.

He rushes forward,
Arm risen high,
Slams it down along the worthless blade of my knife.
I watch his forearm split open,
Skin and muscle divide,
He asks me for a penny before he runs into the night.
Did I just assist in some messed-up suicide?

"I'm sorry, I'm sorry," he screams into the dark.
He's hiding in the bushes,
Trying to keep his arm from splitting apart.
We rush him inside, his blood flowing freely,
God, is he going to die with this messed up feeling?

Screaming for help as we go, into the bathroom we rush him,
lest he bleeds on the cheap carpet of the dorm floor.
I wonder how much blood has been spilled here before.

Splatters on the mirror
Drops congeal on the floor
Someone get a towel!
God, what is this happening for?

The camera lens shutters,
flashes illuminate the night,
Documenting this nightmare,
What the hell is wrong with this guy?
Black and white flashes of a situation filled gray
His blood seemed much colder then, darker, and
fake.

There's banging on the door now.
It's the campus police.
God, he's bleeding all over the place.

My clothes stained with crimson,
My mouth filled with paste,
I don't know how to answer these questions they
raise.
Can we please just go back now, and let me hit
erase, erase, erase?

Erase his bloody handprints from the side of that
sink,
No, it would have been better if he'd just
bloodied my face.
Broken me in that stairwell,
But he'd have been alright,
Is it even possible to trade a life for a life?
He can take mine now,
Of that I am fully sure,
No longer willing to defend,

innocence I've already had shattered so many times before.

He told them I was some crazy girlfriend,
Someone who followed him home,
Thank God for the friend who set the record straight.
They stitched him up just fine, admitted him to some local place.
His parents pulled him from school,
And I never crossed that path again.

Momma said don't think about it,
But I don't know how that works,
Every time I close my eyes, the crazy look of his hurts.
What made him choose himself that night, instead of hurting me?
I still don't understand why I was the one who got to go free.

Decades have gone by now,
Fueled by life's frantic pace.
Time gets so funny,
I question that moment in space.
I wonder if he is a fragment,
Of some random drugged-up night.
Memories of him surface,
Like some drunken strobe light.

But I have to remember,
Somewhere there is a guy,
Who documented it all,
In vivid black and white.

Southern Road

Walking the road that I grew up on, birds singing, rooster crowing despite it being noon. I guess even he is slow going these days. The wind playing with the leaves, gently swaying tops but not enough to reach me down here. Sun is warm on my skin, but the air hasn't turned suffocatingly humid yet. Still remnants of "winter" (ha, what passes for winter around here) in the air. It's not yet threatening to drown me.

Walking past the places I played as a child. A red gate, long since removed. An old semi-trailer, locked but sure to contain massive treasures, had we only been able to get inside, pine trees cut and laid to construct a makeshift cabin we dreamt of spending days in, but abandoned after a few days of high humidity and getting caught with axes and saws we weren't permitted to use.

Smashing plastic lighters with rocks to watch them shatter and pop. Tromping through woods that hid a gorgeous lake, full of wild turkeys, turtles, and snakes. Falling in and changing clothes, like our parents wouldn't notice we came home different. But if they did, they never said a word. The path of least resistance makes more sense to me now. Back then, I just assumed I must somehow be cleverer than they were. Of course, at that age, who doesn't know everything?

Crunching of gravel beneath my feet, throwing rocks in some test of our agility in escaping those granite missiles, and in maintaining the façade of a grinning face when one struck its mark, leaving a massive welt that developed into a purple, green, and yellow mess of a bruise. It always got shown off like you'd survived storming the beaches of Normandy. Man, we were stupid, but the ant beds weren't going to stir themselves.

Worth Less

You don't have to settle for
Whatever this is –
You don't have to wait for him
to tell you who you get to be today –
He doesn't even see you
You're just a trophy on display
Random remnants of something once beautiful
Broken in pieces by a man filled with hate
You don't deserve this –
Don't you know how this story ends?
No happy endings
No one to pretend
You had so much light once
Your laugh filled the room
He's broken you of that now
You dare not speak out of turn
What would it matter –
There's nothing of value you could say
He's stomped on your heartstrings
They no longer play
Where once was a melody
Now, there is nothing once more
Empty and broken
Beaten and alone
Girl, you don't deserve this -

This isn't your home

There's beauty in brokenness
But you won't find it here
I know you're scared to leave –
Don't know who else would care
He tells you you're worthless
And you tend to agree
But there's beauty beneath
all these turbulent waves
and you are worth far more
than the less he sees

Busybody Jiggle-Butt

Everyone who called me that is dead
Overdose
Drown in vomit
Can't remember your own name
Sure, can't remember mine
Once upon a drug-induced haze
But you saw ME
You knew me
You celebrated who I was
The endless energy that never stopped
My happy jiggle that wiggled whenever I walked up the stairs
Society's throw-aways pulling me out of my hell

Most clearly seen by those the world refuses to look at
Outcasts with their hearts on their sleeve
People the world screams, "THROW AWAY!"
Druggies
Drunks
Dealers
Punks
The "worst" this world has to offer, always saw the very best in me

Loved

"A kingdom for a kiss upon your shoulder."
"I've seen your naked, and I don't mean without
clothes."

The soundtrack of my life isn't filled with
music,
but with beautiful phrases that fill my heart like
a song.
With promises that I'm fully seen and have been
loved in this place.
Where no one takes advantage –
or hopes to gain more of me
other than just sharing a moment of my space.

"J'adore tu, Aurelie"
"I'd walk a lot farther than across this living
room,
for a lot less than a cup of coffee for you"

Lyrics to such a beautiful tune –
one that plays again and again,
Snippets of love that touched me for a season,
Simply "because I like you and don't want
anything from you,"
These moments carry on,

well beyond their time and place.
Love notes likely long forgotten,
by the lips through which they passed,
Yet frozen for eternity, written on my heart,
bouncing in my mind,
Keeping such sweet, sweet time.

"Sissonville2056" or any such variation
Promises of some vague tomorrow
Some other time, Some far-off place
My heart will be held in that kindly embrace.
A place where I have been loved
beyond simple face value –

Unable to grasp it, until years had long past,
Maybe that's the only place it truly exists.
Whatever the case,
I'm grateful for such words,
The love they've poured into me,
The hurt that they've cured.

The world shouts its insults, but I no longer hear,
Those lies that it tells me,
The fear it hopes to instill.
I remember the melody, of love from the past,
And know that my heart has found its true rest.

Follower

Did you know I'd be so much trouble,
before you died for me?
Did you know I'd break your heart,
long after you'd set me free?
Did you see those years of darkness,
and all my sorted sin?
Did you know I'd hurt so many,
before my heart would ever let you in?
Did you hear my heart's plotting,
before you went to that grave?
Did you see how much it was hurting?
Is that what you died to save?
How could you have seen me,
and love me anyway?
The dirty stains of my broken past,
surely can't be washed away.

The stench of it all follows me,
like a perfume I can't wash off.
"You can't escape it"
"You're too far lost"
"No one wants you"
"You aren't worth the cost"
"Your death would be welcome"
"You'd be out of the way,

all your madness ended…"
That's the loop that played most days.

But the lies didn't win out,
You had much more in store.
You filled up my brokenness,
with hopes of so much more.
"Be strong and courageous"
"Be still and abide"
"Don't you know you are worthy?"
This is why, my Savior died.
Chains have been broken,
and captive hearts set free.
Lord, I know it's not lip service
because you've done it for me.

You woke up my dead heart,
got it beating once more,
Thank you for redemption, forgiveness,
and everything that life with you has in store.

Wanted

You were in that stairwell
I know you saved us both that night.
You've walked with me
through every single one
of my dirty, broken roads
and self-indulgent, dark nights.
You held my hand
as I destroyed the life
that you had planned for me.
I see your fingerprints all over my past –
You've connected every dot
that you were there to place –
You've created this beautiful photo
out of the things I wanted so badly to erase.
You were in each story -
As I know you'll always be –
Thank you, LORD, for never giving up on me.

Not Alone

Yes, there is sadness,
But you'll also see such peace.
Yes, my tears flow freely,
But that doesn't imply my hope deceased.

I need not pretend that I'm okay,
In order to represent you well.
You never promised me lack of sorrow,
Just that I'd never go alone through this hell.

So, through these tears I will follow,
Where you may lead.
Because I trust you more than the emotions,
that accompany all this pain.

For you've known greater darkness,
No stranger to the pain,
You know what it's like to be forsaken,
And you chose it anyway.

So, I will follow gladly,
No matter where my path leads,
Because I trust my Savior,
Who always walks next to me.

Let Me Grieve

I don't want to be distracted
Please let me feel this pain
I don't want to bottle it up
For some therapist to later have to explain

I need to cry these awful tears
Please don't tell me to dry my face
I need to experience some space to grieve
Not have to put on some brave show

I need permission to be weak today
So that one day I'll be strong
Not shackled to old trauma
And all that once went wrong

I need permission to feel this pain
No matter how it looks
Please don't ask me to pretend
Or to pretty up my looks

Don't ask me to hide my heartache
Please don't tell me it's okay
Because one day it might be
But today is not that day

Don't teach me I have to stay strong
With some plastered-on stage face
Let me weep and mourn and lose my mind
If that is what it takes

Don't ask me to walk into tomorrow
With this anchor around my waist
For it will drown me beneath the waves
Of so much unprocessed grief

Give me space to experience it
Don't ask me to be well
Let me explore my sorrow
So, I don't have to remain tied to this particular hell

Let me miss the life I once had
Or the one that will never be
Let me feel the pain of missing those
Who are no longer here with me

Let me grieve these losses
Because one day I'll look back with joy
And be able to see only beauty
In every page of this broken story

Lump

Darkened waves roll across you once again,
But you just smile at us and continue to pretend.
You helped me through some of life's darkest stuff,
But you never once indicated, you'd end your life in that truck.

Your energy was endless, or so it always seemed,
Your kindness and your laughter,
lifted up the weakest parts of me.
You never issued judgement,
Just ridiculously compassionate care.
You saw through our masks,
And always patiently met us there.
You showed up in a heartbeat,
You always went above,
Never afraid to wear your heart on the sleeve,
Tempered with so much love.

But the happy face we saw,
Covered up so much pain,
Never wanting to be a burden,
You stood along on that range.

You covered it with laughter,
And light and so much love,
All the while your soul sunk deeper,
Into that endless maddening void.

You even called to say goodbye.
I struggle with that to this day,
How could we have been so selfish?
We blindly missed your pain.

Did you want someone to save you?
Would you have stuck around,
If one of us had truly seen your pain,
And been eager to get you out?

I've considered it a million times since then,
Always wondering if we could have changed your fate.
Stormed into your darkness,
And liberated you from hell's gate.

But even in retrospect, none of us saw,
The depth of your pain.
A master at hiding it, dulling it down,
Until you no longer could,
Until that huge heart of yours failed.

I will always miss you,
And wish I'd done more,

To rush into your darkest places,
And drag you out that door.

I'll never forget the gentle way you loved us,
Always so patient and so kind,
Never hesitated to come when needed,
You gave us so much,
Just wish we had to opportunity to give back.

So now I actively look,
For those still trapped in the dark,
Unafraid to go in there,
Unafraid of what is hard.
Unwilling to let another give up on this life,
Because I know despite our heartache,
Hope always remains,
Sometimes we just need reminding,
Sometimes we just need a friendly face.
To walk into the darkness,
To help light the way,
The way you did for others,
Is now how I spend my days.
Loving and seeing and offering hope,
Never leaving anyone to walk these roads alone.

Life can have beauty,
Despite all of its pain.
Our lives become beacons,
Lighting the way in the rain.

Offering hope,
Lighting the path,
Revealing you aren’t alone,
No matter what lies the darkness tries to pass.
Hope still exists here,
Even to this day,
Your absence inspires me,
To live out my love in every way.

Dreamer

Are dreamers born of people
or are they simply made
by the tempting whispers of silence
and all that this world takes?
If hardships hadn't happened
and lovers never lied
would I still be a dreamer
or would I live some other life?
Do the people from the past
haunt you to this day?
Do they sneak up behind you
just when you thought they'd gone away?
Are you trapped by their hold on you?
Or do you just merely ignore
the constant voice of reason
pounding softly on your heart's door?

Seventeen

Seventeen is blissful when you cannot see the past
No awareness of the future to stop you in your tracks
Life seems so much lighter then
More willingness to care
Nothing quite like seventeen
when you're breathing in all that youthful air

Full of selfish ambition
Unable to comprehend,
what one day it will all mean
Oblivious to consequences,
let's just call it Seventeen.

But actions result in permanence
You'll carry throughout your life
Decision you took so lightly
Come roaring back inside
Threatening to overwhelm you
You struggle to catch your breath
You can't understand why it's happening
You never connect the past
You continue to walk in blissful ignorance
Let's just call it Seventeen.

Jose Lied

It used to take a bottle of Cuervo,
To give me the courage to dive in,
To the broken mess inside of me,
That darkness without end.
Too afraid to open the door sober,
Not even a little crack,
That mess would overwhelm me,
Releasing madness, I couldn't take back.

Jose held my hand,
Each time I wanted to venture in,
He tempered my vision and understanding,
And introduced me to his life-long friends.
New substances to dull the pain,
To shut off the voices in my head,
Ignoring the torment inside,
But not understanding why,
the storm kept spilling out of me.

What used to help now hindered,
I couldn't access the mess,
The decay slowly festered,
Building until finally it reached its crest.
It spilled into my every day,
Nothing was left unscathed,

Destroying anything good I held,
Causing "friends" to turn away.
I'd long since lost the key,
I'd slipped into that lock,
Years and years before,
That damn door now was stuck.
No idea where to find a locksmith,
I struggled on my knees,
Asking for forgiveness and direction,
I pleaded with God to guide me.
But the answers didn't come,
No illumination fell on me,
Until my heart lie shattered,
In all my broken memories.

And one day I looked over,
And saw He'd left a key,
With a note that said He would,
Always walk in there with me.
So, I ventured into that darkness,
Afraid of what I might see,
Shame rolled across the walls,
Like some messed up menagerie.

But the moment I turned,
And faced it with the light,
It wasn't nearly as big,
As the space I'd given it in my mind.

He told me He loved me,
And that He'd been there all along,
Waiting for my wayward heart,
To find its way back home.

He showed me each time,
He'd brought me out of the grip of death,
Where each prayer someone prayed for me,
Kept me from the depths.

There's still a mess inside of me,
But I am learning to swing open the doors,
And let the light that cleanses everything,
Work within me to restore,
All the awful brokenness,
And shame and pain and sin.
All off its being wash clean,
He does it again and again.

Each time, we go a little deeper,
Into the depth of my mind,
But He always walks before me,
His love is just so kind.
He showed me the path to healing,
And to trusting Him alone,
Now there isn't much that scares me,
Because I never walk alone.

I'm Sorry

I never meant to hurt you,
Or cause you any pain,
But I didn't understand that,
Loving someone was more than just a game.

I'd met too many players,
Experts in their field,
To understand not everyone,
Would try to take advantage of the way I feel.

So, when you said you loved me,
And you'd never turn away,
I assumed you were like the others,
Saying what you thought you'd need to say.

I never understood,
You'd might see me for myself,
Never quite grasped the fact,
You might really want to help.

My youth-tinted glasses,
Refused to let me see,
Any hope of a future,
Any promise of dependability.

I’m sorry I never saw you,
As well as you saw me,
I didn’t mean to hurt you,
Or diminish such incredible beauty.

I’m grateful I did not cause you,
To give up on finding love’s mark,
Thank you for always pouring into,
My stupid, childish heart.

I’ll always be grateful,
For the way, you opened my eyes,
To the possibility of greater things,
I’d never before felt inside.

Nothing New to Say

Childish versions of these
grown up thoughts
filled with so much pain

Communication stagnant
at that young age
unable to process into the
future until I address
the mess

State-dependent learning
like a stroke survivor
having to learn it all again

40 years old now and
still trying to learn
from my mistakes

Slow Motion

Starting over isn't easy
feels like moving in reverse
but I'm so determined
to break free of this
generational curse

Hiding all our trauma
Holding on to the pain
None of it betters tomorrow
Or changes this sad refrain

Fighting as a child
Looking for some fingerhold
To cling to in this cold, dark place
This abyss is not my home

Women

Women, lift not the weight of the world,
but of the hurting woman beside you
Help her hold it all together
Give her a safe place to rest
See yourself in her mirror image
You know what it's like to be cast out
Look into her soul and refuse to look away
Show her she's not alone
At least not today
Build her up, help hold her load –
You may be the only one
Who ever steps toward her
In that kind of love.

Risk

There is a risk involved in everything
Every time you share a smile
Every time you shed a tear
You are opening yourself up to hurt

Some people tread slowly through life
Avoiding the closeness risk brings
Side-stepping the things, they can't understand
Turning away from those who care too much
those who stay too long, those who hold too
tightly

There is never an easy way to love
You cannot approach it cautiously
It will not wait for you to arm yourself
It does not care if you turn away
It is everywhere, it is in everything
And it is beauty

www.ingramcontent.com/pod-product-compliance
Lightning Source LLC
Chambersburg PA
CBHW051751130826
49812CB00033B/1093
9789357212144